DOGS THROUGHOUT HISTORY™

The Story of the Beagle

Martha Mulvany

The Rosen Publishing Group's
PowerKids Press™
New York

For bad dogs everywhere, especially Guido and Pipo.

Published in 2000 by The Rosen Publishing Group, Inc.
29 East 21st Street, New York, NY 10010

First Edition

Book design: Danielle Primiceri

Photo credits: Cover © A. Schmidecker 1979/FPG International, p. 4 © Archive Photos; p. 7 © Villa Of Casale, Piazza Armerina, Sicily/Silvio Fiore/SuperStock; p. 8 © National Portrait Gallery, London/SuperStock, Pinoteca, Sienna, Italy/SuperStock; p. 11 © Biblioteca Estense, Modena/ET Archive, London/SuperStock; p. 12 © Joe McDonald/Animals Animals; p. 15 © Larry Grant 1987/FPG International; p. 16 © The Everett Collection; p. 19 © USDA/APHIS; p. 20 © Tilley, Arthur 1997/FPG International.

Mulvany, Martha, 1973-
    The story of the beagle / by Martha Mulvany.
        p.   cm.— (Dogs throughout history)
    Includes index.
    Summary: Relates the history of the Beagle from ancient Roman times to the twentieth century, describing their roles as hunters, pets, and members of the United States Department of Agriculture Beagle Brigade.
    ISBN 0-8239-5518-4 (lib. bdg.)
    1. Beagle (Dog breed)—History—Juvenile literature. 2 Beagle (Dog breed)—Juvenile literature. [1. Beagle (Dog breed)—Juvenile literature 2. Dogs.] I. Title II. Series.
SF429.B3M85 1998
636.753'7—dc21   98-49410
                                                                                    CIP
                                                                                    AC

Manufactured in the United States of America

Contents

All About the Beagle

Beagles are among the most popular dogs in America today. People love them for their playfulness and intelligence, their cute, cheerful faces, and their long silky ears. Beagles are small and sturdy **hound** dogs. Beagles may be small, but they have the energy and **stamina** to hunt or play for hours. A Beagle can run up to 40 miles an hour. That is faster than some speed limits for cars! Beagles make great pets because they are so smart and active. These special **traits** also made Beagles important to people in the past.

◀ *Beagles are smart and playful dogs.*

Beagles in Ancient Times

The history of the Beagle goes back so many years, people are not sure exactly when it began. Some of the Beagle's **ancestors** lived in the time of the ancient Romans. When the Romans invaded England in the year A.D. 43, they brought small, rabbit-hunting dogs with them. The dogs would sniff around until they smelled a rabbit. Once they caught a scent, they followed it until they found their **prey**. Then, the dogs chased the rabbit into the hunter's open net. The Romans would have had a difficult time finding enough food without the help of their dogs. These important hounds were probably some of the Beagle's earliest relatives.

The Romans kept small Beagle-like dogs to help them hunt. ▶

Royal Beagles

From the 1300s through the 1500s, British kings and queens owned very small Beagles. King Henry VIII had **packs** of Glove Beagles. They were called Glove Beagles because they were small enough to be held in a person's hand. Henry VIII's daughter, Queen Elizabeth I, also kept small Beagles, called Pocket Beagles. The queen liked to watch her **subjects** race with these dogs. Subjects are people who are ruled by the queen. Crowds would gather to watch contests between people and these fast little Beagles.

King Henry VIII and his daughter,
Queen Elizabeth I, owned Beagles.

Farmers' Helpers

In the 1700s, the kings and queens of England did not want tiny Beagles, so Pocket and Glove Beagles became **extinct**. At this time, large hunting hounds were popular among the wealthy. All Beagles might have become extinct if it were not for the average farmers who kept the **breed** alive. Farmers could not afford to buy and feed large dogs, but they could afford a few small Beagles. Like their distant Roman relatives, these Beagles were good rabbit hunters. Farmers were glad to have Beagles help them find food for their families.

In the 1700s, Beagles helped average farmers like these hunt for food. ▶

How a Beagle Hunts

Beagles are pack animals, so they work best in groups. When they hunt, Beagles spread out and search separately for the scent of a rabbit. Beagles have such sensitive noses that they can smell a rabbit hours after it has hopped by. When a Beagle picks up a scent, she will **bay** to alert the other dogs. Then, all of the Beagles run after the scent of the rabbit. Once they find their prey, they howl to tell the hunter where they are. Beagles are very hard workers. They will circle the rabbit as long as it takes for the hunter to arrive.

◀ *The Beagle's great sense of smell is what makes her a great hunter.*

13

Beagles Are Beautiful

The Beagles that lived in the past did not always look like the Beagles we see today. Some were much smaller. Others had different colored coats than Beagles do now. In the 1800s, an Englishman named Thomas Johnson decided to breed Beagles. Breeding is when animals produce young. People breed dogs by finding an adult male and an adult female who have certain **qualities**, so they will pass those qualities on to their puppies. Thomas wanted his Beagles to be great hunters. He also wanted them to be beautiful. To breed good-looking dogs, Thomas chose Beagles that had white fur with black and brown markings, and long, rounded ears. Johnson helped to make Beagles the beautiful dogs we see today.

Beagles were bred in the 1800s to be cute, like this Beagle puppy. ▶

Famous Beagles

There have been many famous Beagles. Probably the most famous Beagle of all is Snoopy. Charles M. Schulz created "Peanuts," a popular comic strip about a Beagle named Snoopy and his friends. Snoopy is no hunter, though! Like most pets, he spends his time eating, sleeping, and hanging around with his owner, Charlie Brown.

Lyndon B. Johnson, who was president of the United States from 1963 to 1969, had two Beagles named Him and Her. President Johnson upset Beagle lovers across the country when a reporter photographed him picking up his pets by their ears. President Johnson said the dogs liked it. Other people thought the dogs might be hurt.

◀ *Snoopy is one of the most famous Beagles.*

The Beagle Brigade

The Beagle's great sense of smell is now helping airport officials keep foreign insects and diseases out of the country. The United States Department of Agriculture has trained Beagles to recognize the smell of meat and **citrus** fruit. These items sometimes carry dangerous **bacteria** that can be harmful to people and crops.

A Beagle named Caps, wearing the green vest of the Beagle Brigade, caught 3,500 people carrying illegal food into New York's Kennedy Airport in just one year. To let his trainer know that something is wrong, Caps sits down when he smells illegal foods. Caps's trainer said, "Caps is so cute, people don't mind getting busted!"

Beagles, like this one, help keep illegal food out of our country. ▶

Beagle Heroes

Beagles are very loving and loyal dogs that stand by their owners. In the 1800s, there lived a famous Swiss mountain dog, named **Tschingel**. Unlike most mountain dogs, Tschingel was not large. He was a little Beagle. Tschingel and her owner, W. A. B. Coolidge, climbed 66 mountains together.

Klutz, another loyal Beagle, saved three-year-old Lindsey De Santo's life. In 1992, Lindsey was playing near a rattlesnake in her front yard. Klutz attacked the snake, while Lindsey ran to safety. Days later, Klutz died from the snakebites. Lindsey's family was very grateful to Klutz for saving Lindsey's life. Klutz was a true hero!

◀ *Beagles are very loyal to their owners.*

21

Beagles Today

   Beagles and people have a long history of working together. They have hunted together, climbed mountains together, and protected each other. Probably the most important job a Beagle has today is being a great pet. Beagles enjoy being around people and other pets. They like to play a lot and enjoy plenty of exercise. People need Beagles, too. Friendly and cheerful, Beagles make people feel loved. No wonder these happy hounds are such popular pets today.

Web Sites:

http://kathy.faithweb.com/beaglestuff/
http://www.teleport.com/~canderso/beaglehome.
   html

Glossary

ancestors (AN-ses-turz) Relatives who lived long ago.

bacteria (bak-TEER-ee-uh) Tiny living things that sometimes cause illness or decay.

bay (BAY) A sound between a bark and a howl that hounds make when they find the scent of their prey.

breed (BREED) A group of animals that look very much alike and have the same kind of relatives.

citrus (SIH-trus) Lemons, limes, oranges, grapefruits, and other similar fruit.

extinct (ik-STINKT) To no longer exist.

hound (HOWND) A name for dogs that hunt by scent and usually have short hair and long, drooping ears.

pack (PAK) A group of the same kind of animal hunting or living together.

prey (PRAY) An animal that is hunted and eaten by another animal for food.

qualities (KWA-li-teez) Features that make an individual special.

stamina (STA-mih-nuh) The ability to work or play for a long time.

subjects (SUB-jeks) People who are ruled by someone else.

traits (TRAYTS) Certain qualities of an animal's appearance or behavior.

Tschingel (SHEEN-gul) A famous Swiss mountain Beagle that lived in the 1800s.

Index